How to Resolve Bullying in the Workplace

Stepping out of the Circle of Blame to Create an Effective Outcome for All

Table of Contents

Acknowledgements

I would like to acknowledge the role my parents Marjorie and Derek Sharland played in helping me to see that difficulties in a relationship can be resolved without abuse or lingering resentment. I would also like to thank my partner Jayne for always being open to creating new, exciting ways of dealing with the inevitable challenges an intimate relationship brings.

I would like to thank the many colleagues I have had the pleasure of working alongside on the fascinating journey that is being a mediator and conflict coach, particularly Susie Adams my 'mediation sister' who has always supported, challenged and inspired me since we first worked together in 2000. And of course I would like to thank the participants in mediation and conflict coaching with whom I have worked for giving me the privilege of learning from them how the resolution of any difficult relationship, communication breakdown or other conflict situation is always possible.

Introduction:

Bullying has become an ever-present term in discussions about difficult workplace relationships. We hear that bullying is 'on the rise' and the challenges it poses for organisations can be almost insurmountable.

The literature about bullying is pervaded by aggressive titles suggesting that fighting back, confronting, combating, exposing, defeating, overcoming 'the bully' is the appropriate response, not recognising, it seems, the irony of such titles in that most complaints about bullying suggest aggressive behaviour by the alleged bully as part of the problem.

When you point a finger at someone, always remember there are three fingers pointing back at you - **Anonymous**

The intention of most approaches to bullying seems to be one of getting revenge, 'giving them a taste of their own medicine'. In short, finding, or becoming, a bigger bully to bully the bully.

It is not surprising therefore that the responses to bullying are rarely effective or found to be satisfactory by those affected. No sooner has 'action' been taken, than the accusations become reversed and the original accuser or, at least, those who take up their cause, become the accused.

If you were to do a search on Google for 'bullying punishments' and look at the images section of the results you would see many examples of children and adults who have been deemed to be 'bullies' who have had to stand in public with a large sign in front of them with statements such as "I am a Bully. Honk if you hate bullies" (for a boy of around 10 years old). This mindset that seeks humiliation and shaming of those considered to be bullies is no less bullying than those found 'guilty' and therefore simply perpetuates the very existence of bullying rather than create a better way of responding.

***We cannot solve our problems with the same thinking we used when we created them.* - attributed to Albert Einstein**

My work in the fields of mediation and conflict coaching has given me the privilege of observing the capacity of many people involved in such situations to be able to create a more effective way of responding to the relationship breakdowns and unresolved conflicts that lead to allegations of 'bullying'.

By setting the concept of bullying aside in order to look more deeply into their working relationship and their responses to each other, they have created ways of doing things in their future working relationship that have enabled the problem to be left in the past.

Many will see reflections of known psychological and behavioural theories within the book but I will leave that for them to read into what is written. This book is as much for those who have no interest in, knowledge of, nor use for such theories as it is for those who do.

The book won't provide the answer to all situations where bullying is alleged, but it will provide an approach which is not based on the same thinking used to create the problem in the first place. This is an approach which I have observed working for many people who have resolved their difficulties, including suggestions of bullying behaviour, through mediation and conflict coaching or just through trying a different way to that which presently seems to be the 'normal' way of dealing with bullying allegations.

Chapter 1: The problem with bullying in the workplace and why traditional responses don't work

The problem with bullying in the workplace is that traditional responses to allegations that it is happening require the person who feels bullied and anyone who is helping them with their concerns to 'Prove it!'.

While those who feel bullied may see their experience as 'obviously bullying', there will be others who do not, including of course the person who they consider to be 'the bully'. This expectation of proof of bullying becomes an immediate obstacle in moving forward in any difficult situation or relationship in the workplace.

The various definitions of bullying that can be found in dictionaries or guidelines or in articles online and in the printed press read as if they are very clear. But when used as a basis for assessing whether bullying has taken place they are ambiguously interpreted because of the subjectivity of the perceptions of those involved. It is not a coincidence that in United Kingdom law there is no formal definition of bullying.

Unfortunately there is not just one 'definition' of bullying and so it is very easy for someone to find examples of behaviours that have occurred that they would classify as bullying but others would not. I found a book the other day that listed at least 30 behaviours that were apparently characteristics of 'a bully' and yet many of them could apply to any one of us at different times and in different circumstances.

Examples included:

- Being suspicious

- Giving minimalistic responses when asked 'How are you?'

- Disagreeing with the person who feels bullied

- Being impatient

- Looking to blame

- Being critical of their organisation

I doubt if anyone reading this book could say they have never acted in one or more of these ways.

So are we all bullies? Some of the literature discussing 'bullies' would seem to suggest there are 'bullies' and there are the rest of us, as if the distinction is obvious. This is the consequence when we create stereotypes rather than deal with people as individuals in order to keep our connection with the humanity in each of us.

Those who feel bullied will generally find others who agree with them but may not wish to accommodate the views of those that do not align with their view that they have been bullied, who propose different interpretations of the behaviour of the person seen by them as a bully. In such situations they may say 'everyone agrees' that the person is a bully when it may not be the case.

When I have done group mediations involving allegations of bullying in the workplace by one or more persons there is not general agreement on whether it has occurred when I meet the team members separately, even though some claim there is.

Indeed it is often the case that the person accusing someone else of bullying can be seen by team members as aggressive or harassing in their behaviour because of their persistence with their accusations.

It can be difficult for team members to say this openly as that is seen as betrayal in something not felt to be directly affecting them, although any such situation usually does. In some situations, the isolation and stigmatisation of the person suggested to be 'the bully' could fall just as much within interpretations of the definitions of bullying, and even of discrimination, as the actions they are alleged to have carried out.

This is the bad news in relation to bullying. From the very start of any procedure designed to 'tackle' it by proving it has occurred there is ambiguity for anyone involved, whether the person who feels bullied, the person they see as 'the bully' or any managers or Human Resources officers who are required to deal with it.

The consequence of this is a circle of finger-pointing - blame and accusations and counter-accusations of bullying, incompetence, conspiracy, lack of care, burying of heads in the sand and so very little change, if any, occurs in the majority of cases where bullying is alleged.

Consider the journey an allegation of bullying will usually have to go through:

The person who feels bullied is required to give proof that it has happened. Even where they have a definition to refer to, their claims that what has happened constitutes bullying are very hard to prove and very easily challenged. Let's take an example:

Bullying may be characterised as:

Offensive, intimidating, malicious or insulting behaviour, an abuse or misuse of power through means that undermine, humiliate, denigrate or injure the recipient.

Bullying or harassment may be by an individual against an individual (perhaps by someone in a position of authority such as a manager or supervisor) or involve groups of people. It may be obvious or it may be insidious. Whatever form it takes, it is unwarranted and unwelcome to the individual.

From: 'Bullying and harassment at work' - ACAS Guide for Employees (UK)

While the phrases used sound clear it is very hard to 'prove' that such things have happened. If they were not so hard to prove then countless bullying allegations would not have ended in frustration for those who feel bullied because no-one seemed to believe them or felt able to agree that their evidence proved it.

Proving that someone's intention is to 'undermine, humiliate, denigrate or injure' is very difficult to do and easily argued to be a 'misinterpretation' or 'seeing the worst in someone', or   being 'oversensitive'.

To receive such comments can be immensely stressful for the person who feels bullied as it feels as if they are not believed and, as a consequence, that they have no hope of addressing their concerns and no support in doing so.

Something that can feel reassuring at the start of their complaint - a definition of bullying to refer to - can then become the biggest obstacle to proving it has occurred!

For the person affected this focus on proving bullying has occurred but a sense that they are not believed can feel like the people in place to support their complaint are ineffective, incompetent, siding with 'the bully', 'in it together' with others in senior positions, particularly if the person they see as a bully is their manager.

This is where the circle of blame begins. At first there is just the accusation of bullying by another person - a team member or a manager or other colleague. But eventually it can lead to accusations of others in the organisation conspiring to prevent the issue being dealt with. Further accusations of 'cover up' or 'whitewash' follow.

This perception then becomes an expected 'norm' in the narrative about responses to bullying. Articles are written suggesting the reasons why managers, CEO's, leaders 'ignore bullies' as if there is a clear sign above each person who is a bully, and senior managers and HR officers ignore the sign.

And yet, in my experience of providing mediation or conflict coaching in such disputes that is rarely, if ever, the case. The perception arises from the almost impossible task of 'proving' that bullying has occurred and the challenge that those investigating face in carrying through the investigation of the allegation with any likelihood of an unambiguous outcome.

To get a wider view of the dynamics in the situation let's move on to the person accused of being a bully to see how their experience keeps the situation within a circle of accusations and counter-accusations.

The person who is accused of bullying will almost always reject the suggestion and may feel angry, offended, and dismissive that it should even be made. Some people may say 'Well they would wouldn't they!', but this is to see them as guilty before any proof has been shown to exist - and to buy in to the idea that 'proving bullying has occurred' is the only available response to such situations.

Where someone who alleges bullying and those who seek to support them take this view and approach, the process again fails as it expects the alleged 'bully' to be treated in a way which is *an abuse or misuse of power through means that undermine, humiliate, denigrate or injure the recipient.* - to use one of the many definitions of bullying available.

Labeling someone as 'a bully' without proof and treating him or her as one prior to any formal hearing which finds it to be so could easily be seen to fall into a category of bullying behaviour such as a misuse of power, or an intent to humiliate or denigrate the recipient. .

Sometimes there can be persistent attempts by people who feel bullied to act in ways that could be seen as designed to undermine, humiliate, denigrate or injure the person they have accused. Gossiping about them, complaining to other staff in terms that are abusive and critical, not speaking to them when present, and others. As a consequence the person accused can feel both unfairly treated because of the apparent hypocrisy in the allegation but also may make counter-allegations of bullying against their original accuser.

And so the circle of accusatory finger-pointing continues but you can probably see how this is very unlikely to lead to a resolution. Instead it is most likely to lead to a bitter, festering entrenchment by all involved and a consequent criticism by both the person who feels bullied and the person they accuse (although the distinctions are starting to blur at this stage) of those managing the situation for not fulfilling a duty of care towards them.

Many who read this who have been tasked with managing allegations of bullying will recognise this 'dead end' and the bad atmosphere that lingers in any work environment where it has occurred.

So, to continue the journey, let's look further into the place of those involved in investigating the allegations or overseeing the situation, such as a manager of the people involved or an HR officer brought in to deal with the situation, and how they also get caught up in the circle of blame and accusations that arise.

As outside observers of the situation, it is very difficult for a manager or HR officer to come to a clear view about whether bullying has occurred or not. And yet in order to take any action they have to be clear, just as any Police officer would have to be clear there is sufficient evidence that a crime has been committed if

14

they are to pursue criminal prosecution of someone for an alleged crime.

Managers can't immediately take the side of the person who originally complains, and it can, at first, be difficult to maintain that impartiality when an account is given of the behaviours of the person accused of bullying and the interpretations of those behaviours by the person affected.

Managers also have to hear the view of the person accused and often they will find them defensive and feeling offended that the allegation has been made. There will be justifications of their actions through quoting examples of inappropriate behaviour by the person who has alleged the bullying, examples of lack of performance and suggestions that the bullying allegation is a way of both avoiding dealing with their low performance and a way of justifying it. These responses become a minefield of subjective perceptions with little chance of ever establishing the 'facts' of the situation which are needed to come to a view about whether bullying has occurred or not.

As a result they are rarely able to satisfy the expectations of either person involved in the situation:

The person who feels they are being bullied feels let down and that the accused colleague has been 'let off'. They feel they are not believed or that the investigators have conspired with the person who is alleged to be the bully either because he or she is a manager or if not in a superior role, because he or she has 'charmed them' or found some other way of refuting the claims (another common characterisation in literature about 'people who are bullies' is that they are able to charm others so that their 'real' character is not seen).

The person accused of bullying remains dissatisfied with the outcome and will turn their anger on those investigating because they want to clear their name and get on with their role as manager or other role, but instead there is no decisive outcome to the investigation so it hangs over them like a dark cloud.

Thus the managers or HR officers tasked with dealing with the allegation stand accused of incompetence, apathy, denial, bias, conspiracy and a failure to fulfill their duty of care.

And this all arises because of the need to 'prove' bullying has occurred within most organisations' approaches to difficult working relationships.

The failure of this approach is not because of failure on the part of those who seek to use it; it is down to the fact that it is an ineffective way of responding to difficult behaviours and relationships in the workplace. It tries to condense the problem into a 'one-size fits all ' concept.

The concept of 'a bully' that follows from this approach places all cause of any difficulties within a working relationship in one person, rather than recognise that a workplace relationship is a combination of interactions and subjective interpretations of those interactions, unique to those involved in the relationship.

Bullying is not like a crime such as rape or murder or theft where a particular action has been carried out by one or more persons, proof is found to establish that it occurred and punitive action taken. There are far clearer definitions within law against which to assess whether they have occurred or not (unlike bullying which has no legal definition, for good reason).

The concept of bullying tries to encapsulate an ongoing relationship, subjectively interpreted and contributed to by more than one person rather than a more clearly defined event such as theft, rape, murder, and so proof is almost impossible to achieve.

But within this recognition of the ineffectiveness of proving bullying has occurred resides the possibility for breaking out of the circle of blame and accusations that lead to dissatisfaction all round the circle. This possibility is available to all involved in such situations if they are able to do one thing:

To let go of the focus on 'bullying'!

As I will discuss in the next chapter, the ways in which I have seen people resolve workplace disputes where originally there have been accusations of bullying and harassment have been where the term 'bullying' retreats from the discussion.

When this happens, a more useful, detailed discussion relevant to the unique circumstances and perceptions of those involved can occur, enabling, and expecting them to create their own answers to their difficult working relationship.

Chapter 2: How bullying situations are resolved - observations from Mediation and Conflict Coaching

Mediation is a process that doesn't look to establish proof, who is 'right' and who is 'wrong', who is telling lies and who is telling the truth. Its approach is like saying: 'Ok, what has happened so far is not working for you both so what is going to mean it works better in the future?'. It doesn't focus on one person to see what they have done 'wrong', it helps all involved to look at the relationship and interactions between them with an aim of supporting them in working together to create different ways of doing things in the future. It doesn't ignore that there may be concerns about engaging in the process or that there are difficult feelings that both may be carrying in relation to the situation. But the expectation is that participants are using mediation as a tool to help them move forward from their damaged working relationship. It serves no other purpose.

Participants in mediation may have views about whose fault the problem is or what the other person does that is wrong but mediation isn't able to vindicate them, nor to have it proven about them if they are accused of something, such as 'being a bully'.

Because of this approach in mediation, if someone says. 'Joe is a bully', as a Mediator I don't say. 'Can you prove it?' I'd say, 'So what is it Joe does that leads you to describe him as a bully?'

At first it may seem like that's asking the same question in a different way, but its purpose is entirely different. If the response is: 'He shouts so loud and embarrasses me when I get something wrong. He's trying to humiliate me', the follow up question will not be: 'Can you prove it, do you have witnesses who will confirm what you say?', it will be something like: 'So if you get something wrong, how would you like Joe to do things differently that won't feel like he's trying to humiliate you?'

The focus is always on creating a way of doing things differently and better in the future if what has happened has been ineffective or upsetting or just 'not working' however that is meant, in the past. The focus is not on recrimination or seeking punishment to be meted out as retribution.

So following on from the last question the answer may be something like:

'I wish he'd just accept that people make mistakes and if it's a problem for him, that he helps me with fixing it without making such an embarrassing fuss about it all. Why does he have to shout and scream and draw so much attention to it? Does he never make mistakes? '

So you will notice they are not now talking about whether bullying has happened or not, they are discussing the specifics of what happened, how it felt to experience it, what they would like to be done differently. They are laying the foundations for making changes that will work better for them in the future.

If Joe is present at the mediation he will have a chance to hear how what he has done was experienced by the first person, let's call him Bob, and learn what he would like for the future. Additionally, if Joe were present, what is said would be said to him by Bob, rather than about him, so that a discussion is more likely to ensue.

Some may think a 'bully' won't be interested in listening or doing things differently but if it is an alternative to a process where they have to defend themselves against an accusation of bullying with the accompanying confusion and stress described in the last chapter, it is more likely to be considered a better option to engage in such a discussion.

Such a belief about 'the bully' - that they will not want to engage in such a process - is rarely explored but it will often be found to be an inaccurate assumption. It is a common occurrence that once we ascribe a label to someone it is difficult to see in them anything that does not fit our definition of that label. This is the basic flaw in all stereotyping and applies just as much to the term 'bully' as it does to other labels.

If for any reason there is not a mediation meeting between Bob and Joe so that Joe is not able to hear what Bob has to say, then there can be an exploration with Bob about how he can communicate by some other means to Joe what he would like to happen and for him to be aware of. Again, it is not a communication that is accusatory and so Joe is less likely to dismiss it or just defend against what is said than if it is purely accusatory and suggesting he is 'a bully'.

This is an example of how someone who feels bullied can respond differently and in a way that is more likely to help the situation than one that is more likely to entrench it and reduce the chances of a better outcome.

Unfortunately when avoiding or allocating blame is the focus, such an idea can be described as 'victim blaming' because it suggests the person who felt bullying has occurred has done something 'wrong' by not communicating in this way originally and so is being 'blamed' for the difficulties that have arisen. Where this view is taken, it can mean the approach is opposed and the situation stays within the 'Prove it!' approach and the circle of blame continues.

For a situation where only one person is being supported because the other is not involved for some reason, Conflict Coaching can be helpful to enable the person to consider what they see as a better way forward and how to address the issues they want to with the other person.

The situations where mediation and conflict coaching can be a useful option are where managers or HR officers are expected to carry out an investigative process into the allegations of bullying. As a result the people involved may not feel comfortable having such discussions with someone they know is also investigating them in parallel with the discussion they are having because it can seem like a conflict of roles and a conflict of interests.

But it may not have to be via mediation or conflict coaching that such discussions are enabled. Just understanding and implementing a different approach can be enabled by any of those involved and we will look at how to take such discussions forward from the perspective of the person who feels bullied, the person accused of bullying and any manager or HR officer tasked with dealing with the issue respectively, in the next 3 chapters.

Chapter 3: So you feel you are being bullied? What can you do?

If you feel you are being bullied you may be aware of procedures in your workplace that allow for a complaint of bullying or harassment to be made. This book is not suggesting you shouldn't make use of such procedures, just that you be aware that they may be difficult to carry through to a conclusion you are happy with.

You may feel very sure that you are being bullied but it is often very difficult to prove this to be so as others may interpret someone's behaviour differently to how you do, particularly the person you feel is 'the bully'. As discussed in the first chapter it may be that managers or HR officers at your organisation are expected to carry through such procedures on your behalf but because they have to have clear proof of something that is often very difficult to prove, because it is ambiguously defined and the experience is subjective, they may not be able to help you in the way you hope.

So in order to provide alternative responses that you can use alongside such procedures or instead of them if you choose to, this chapter is designed to help you consider other ways of approaching the situation.

As has been mentioned previously a way that has been effective within mediation situations (although it does not have to occur within mediation) is to look in more detail at the actions or behaviours that you see as being 'bullying'.

First of all, list the things that the person you believe is bullying you does. Just write them down as a list of actions or behaviours such as 'They shout at me for no reason' or 'They pick on me in meetings' or 'They undermine me in front of colleagues' or whatever other actions or behaviours you feel are bullying.

Once the list is complete, go through it and decide which ones are definitely true and which ones are your interpretation. This may prove challenging as you may want to see all of them as 'true' but here are some examples that fit each category:

Definitely true:

- They shout at me when I get things wrong. (If the person definitely speaks louder when you have made a mistake you can be pretty clear about this)

- They swear at me (be clear they are swearing at you rather than just swearing - such as 'You are a bloody idiot' rather than ' Oh bloody hell!')

- They bang the table in meetings I have with them (are these meetings just with you or when others are present as well? If the latter, decide why you feel the behaviour is directed at you rather than at everyone, or is it an expression of frustration not directed at anyone in particular that you would prefer they didn't do?)

Possibly interpretation:

- They try to undermine me in meetings

- They stop me from getting promotions

- They keep information from me to make me look stupid

- They think I am incapable so only give me menial tasks

The reason these are in the 'Possibly interpretation' category is because you are presuming to know why someone has done something, which, unless they have actually told you that is their motivation, you can only be speculating that that is their reason for doing what they have done.

If it isn't clear which actions or behaviours go in which category, don't worry as it is just to get you thinking about what the person does that upsets you or concerns you instead of focusing on whether they are or are not a bully.

To clarify, this is not about deciding whether you are right or wrong in your interpretation, this isn't about proving that but to consider which things have definitely happened and which may be an interpretation.

Remember this approach is about moving away from proving or disproving that bullying has occurred, and towards looking at the detail of what has happened that is of concern to you so that you can address those behaviours and actions with the other person. It is also to explore your own response to those things happening so that you can support yourself effectively if they happen again.

Now that you have your list of actions or behaviours that you are concerned by in the other person, consider to what extent you have communicated with the other person about them?

So for example, to what extent has it been possible to say something like the following about actions that have concerned you:

- You shout at me when I get things wrong.

Can you try to keep your voice lower if I get things wrong? I don't need to be shouted at and it doesn't really contribute to improving things if you do. It can feel like you are trying to humiliate me. Whether you are or not I don't know but it would just help if you spoke instead of shouting.

- You swear loudly over what I think are the smallest things and I think you are being aggressive when you do that.

Maybe you normally swear in how you express yourself, but it doesn't really help me to understand what you are concerned about. Can you let me know without swearing when you are concerned about something and I'll try to remedy the situation or, ideally, we can discuss together what we can do to sort it out. Swearing doesn't help me with that so for both of us to move forward can you bear that in mind?

- You bang the table when we have meetings and I'm worried you are going to become violent.

Why do you bang the table? It concerns me when you do that and, like with the swearing I don't see how it helps. Can you let me know what you want without doing that?

(Note here the important difference in the last question between saying '*Can* you let me know what you want without doing that?' which is a clear request, and '*Can't* you let me know what you want without doing that?' which can sound more like a criticism).

Consider to what extent you have addressed the person in this way.

Now consider some common ways of addressing the same issues which are less effective:

- You're always shouting.

- You are aggressive and you swear all the time.

- You are violent in meetings.

These ways of expressing a concern are less effective as they are still accusatory.

When something is expressed as an accusation, it immediately makes it less likely the person is going to want to listen to what is said and they are more likely to become defensive. It is also what makes it possible that the accusation itself is seen as aggressive and therefore seems hypocritical to the person spoken to when it comes from someone accusing them of being a bully.

To state things in this more accusatory way is where approaches to bullying often start to go wrong and become 'stuck'.

The other ineffective aspect of the above statements is that some of them suggest what is said is a fact when it is a belief or an opinion or an inaccurate generalisation.

'You are violent in meetings.' is likely to lead to a dismissive response if the person has 'just' banged a table rather than been directly violent towards you. If you have this kind of concern try to discuss what actually happens and your concern about it rather than label it as 'violent' which is likely to be seen as another accusation and therefore be defended against.

So let's return to one of the original statements and the request that went with it to look at why it helps in moving forward a discussion about improving a difficult workplace relationship:

- You bang the table when we have meetings and I'm worried you are going to become violent.

Request: *Why do you bang the table? It concerns me when you do that and, I don't see how it helps. Can you let me know what you want without doing that?*

When you focus on what has happened and then refer to it and make a request for what you would like you are much more likely to get a co-operative response and create a shared decision about how to improve a situation than if you accuse someone of bullying without giving them a chance to discuss it with you and understand how you have seen it that way

If possible, you can also explore why the person does things in the way they do so that you are open to hearing from them their view on what they have done, rather than criticise it or assume a negative intention.

If you have made previous attempts to communicate but your statements have been 'complaints' about them then, again, it is possible they will have been defensive rather than co-operative in their response. So if you have tried before, consider whether you have done so in the way described above that remains open to their view and invites co-operation, or whether it has been accusatory and critical.

This can be challenging if you are already feeling intimidated or uneasy in the presence of the person - but its purpose is to enable you to take steps to address your concerns in a way that is assertive rather than aggressive and accusatory. It seeks an answer from the person about what they have done and why they have done it in order to help you both understand the situation better and start to create a different, more constructive way forward.

Bullying complaints rarely, if ever, allow for that possibility as the focus is just on proving that bullying has or has not occurred and so an open discussion between you and the other person of what in particular has happened and why they acted that way is not possible within that process. Indeed most approaches lead to the two people being kept apart and so the assumptions about what has happened and why remain unexplored, and the reasons are assumed to be negative and malicious.

As mentioned earlier, some people object to the approach suggested in this book because they see it as 'victim blaming'. But this comes from a perspective which says, 'If we are not blaming the 'bully' we must be blaming the 'victim'.

The point is this is not about looking for blame in anyone, its purpose is to help you stand back from the situation and look in on what it is that is actually upsetting you and causing you concern rather than be 'caught up' in it and feel the only way out is to allege that the other person is a bully.

You have every right to pursue that allegation via whatever procedures are available to you, but the reason this book has been written is because in many instances of bullying being addressed via a complaint in that way it does not succeed - and as described earlier, most people involved can end up accusing each other of 'failing' in some way, when in fact it is the approach which is ineffective and so it fails to lead to a satisfactory outcome for anyone involved.

Chapter 4: So you are accused of being a bully? What can you do?

If you have been accused of bullying in your workplace it is possible you have felt quite offended or annoyed that the allegation has been made. You may have sought advice about how to defend yourself against the allegation and the process that followed the allegation may have involved you having to meet with someone more senior or an HR officer to discuss it.

The accusation may seem unfair and you may see it as a 'ploy' by someone you don't get along with, such as a colleague you work alongside or someone you manage, to 'get at you' for a reason which you may or may not be aware of. There can be consequences to being accused of bullying that are difficult to manage and worrying with regard to your reputation and what it might mean for the future.

If you have read the previous section written for people who feel bullied you may have seen that this book is not suggesting you don't follow the procedures present within your organisation if it is important and expected that you do so, but as described in the first chapter of the book, be aware that an investigative procedure into whether bullying has occurred or not can be fraught with difficulty because it is so hard to prove, or, perhaps more importantly for you, disprove.

You may feel clear that you have not acted in a way that is 'bullying' and feel confident that an investigative procedure will bear this out, and you may be right. But in the meantime consider what the consequences of the outcome of such an investigation may be, whatever the outcome.

If it is decided you have been bullying a colleague or someone you manage, what will that mean for you? If that possibility concerns you, what may you be able to do now that can help yourself and the situation, and the person who has made the allegation? Below we will look at some ways that might help with that.

If it is decided you have not been bullying a colleague or someone you manage, what will that mean for you? What will the consequences be of such an investigation for you, your colleague who accused you, your work environment? If any of your answers are a concern for you, what could you do now to help yourself, the situation and the person who has made the allegation? (You will perhaps have noticed the questions are the same whatever the outcome).

But there's a third outcome to consider in the situation and it is one which is quite common in workplaces where an allegation of bullying has been made and some kind of investigation has taken place. That is the outcome that comes to no clear conclusion because of the ambiguity of the meaning of bullying and the subjective perceptions of those involved about what has happened. If there is no clear decision about whether you have been bullying a colleague or someone you manage, what will that mean for you?

Again the questions remain the same.

- What could you do now to help yourself?

- What could you do   now to help the situation?

- What could you do now to help the person who has made the allegation that you have bullied them?

If you are open to considering these questions in any situation where an allegation has been made that you have been a bully, whatever the outcome of any investigation into it, then there is a good chance you will be able to move towards a genuine resolution of the situation rather than one in which there is always a bitter taste, an awkwardness in the presence of those involved whether the person who alleged that you are a bully or sometimes the people who have investigated the allegations as well.

Consider this further question within an approach that can help you, the situation and the other person so that you can try to move forward from the difficulties that have occurred previously:

- What would enable you to find out more from the person who sees you as a bully about their reasons for seeing you that way, to find out what it is you've done that they feel was 'bullying'?

It is almost inevitable that you will interpret your behaviours differently to how they have seen them, and seen your intentions differently as well. But to be open to hearing their view rather than simply defend against it (which you are expected to do if you are accused of bullying) can enable a greater understanding of why there is a problem.

You don't have to agree with their interpretation of your actions and behaviours, just to be willing to hear them so that you can try to see their point of view because it helps to inform the creation of a better way forward in the future.

This differs significantly from defending against allegations of bullying because in that process the practice is usually to negate and dismiss any point of view that supports the allegation of bullying. In this approach the openness to the person's view is not in relation to deciding whether your actions and behaviours have or have not been 'bullying', but to the specific things that have happened and how they have interpreted them so that their view can inform a better way of doing things in your working relationship in the future.

So for example, you could ask them: What is it I did that you felt was 'bullying'?

They may say you shouted at them, or you swore or you stood over them when speaking to them in a way they found intimidating, or you ignored them when passing them at work and so they feel you are isolating them, or other actions that can feel upsetting for people for one reason or another.

The important thing is not to dismiss what they say but to try to understand why they interpreted your actions as something unpleasant or malicious or difficult in whatever way they have. You may or may not see why they have interpreted it that way but that is not what is most important.

What does matter is that you find out what would help both of you in the future so that the problem does not occur again.

What would you want from them to help with that? You may wish to ask what they want from you and if it is possible and acceptable to you, you may choose to do it in the future.

If it is not possible for you it is important you say so rather than agree to something you are not comfortable with and so won't be able to sustain as an option. You can explain why the proposal doesn't work for you and then continue to explore other possibilities until you find one or more options that work for both of you. They may have difficulties with proposals you suggest as well in which case you can both explore other options together.

The point is that now you are not engaged in 'proving or disproving' that you are a bully. Instead you are having a discussion about what can improve things in the future but without you having to compromise what you feel is important such as, if relevant, expecting professionalism in terms of performance and conduct in future. They will be able to have a similar approach and expectation of you in such a discussion.

This may sound like a tough challenge and a lot of work - but if you compare it to the time, stress and difficulties associated with defending against an allegation of bullying you may see that it has particular benefits in that it is working to create something useful and constructive for the future rather than to destroy your reputation or theirs within your workplace and possibly beyond that.

Please bear in mind that this is not about becoming 'friends', it is about developing a constructive, forward looking response to past difficulties in your working relationship with the other person (and you will notice I don't call them your 'accuser' as the dynamics of this situation are not accusation-defence but listen-discuss) in order to continue that working relationship in a respectful, professional manner.

The approach can often be considered doubtful in terms of its likelihood of success, usually because of doubts about the other person and their motivations and intentions and capacities. But bear in mind they may have the same concerns about you. In my experience of being a mediator in such situations it is almost always the case that there is an element of doubt about the other person's willingness and motivation - and yet it is frequently so that people still proceed with the process and create a different way of dealing with things in the future.

If it is the case that the other person does not wish to engage in such a discussion described above this does not have to be the end of any chance of moving forward. An individual who is accused of bullying can remain open to hearing the other person's viewpoint even if it does return to just accusations of bullying rather than detail of what has happened. There will usually be some detail within what is said that can be explored further with the person, or even just considered by yourself if they don't wish to talk, in order to create other ways of responding to the person that answer the 3 questions :

- What could you do now to help yourself?

- What could you do now to help the situation?

- What could you do now to help the person who has made the allegation that you have bullied them?

This can be supported by talking the issue through with a facilitator such as a Conflict Coach or someone who is able to remain impartial in their support of you rather than take your side or try to 'fix' the situation for you. But you can even do it yourself if you review the questions within this chapter and create similar ones for yourself that help to reflect on what has happened and how you can support yourself in responding in a way that is open to new ways of developing the working relationship into something more positive.

It only takes one person to end a war, and you're the one. What a perfect set-up! - Byron Katie author of 'Loving What Is'

You may think: 'Why should I try to improve things if they don't want to talk?', and in a way only you can answer that. But bear in mind the benefits for yourself of still trying to do so via this approach even if you are disappointed or even resent that the other person doesn't participate. The potential consequences of only trying the investigation approach have already been outlined so you may wish to try to improve things by yourself in order to pursue a different outcome than that which an investigation often leads to.

It's your choice, because it's your difficult situation.

Chapter 5: So you are managing situations where allegations of bullying have occurred? What can you do?

As a manager or HR officer involved in a situation where there has been an allegation of bullying you probably have a procedure you are expected to follow and that is right and proper as there may be serious misconduct or mistreatment going on for which your organisation has a duty to act.

As stated in the previous chapters written for the other participants in a bullying allegation, this chapter is not suggesting you use the following approach to replace that procedure, but that it be used alongside it, to try to support the possibility of a working relationship continuing and for there to be a useful, constructive resolution for both participants.

As you will probably know, once an investigative procedure into bullying or harassment begins, the long term consequences will frequently be that at least one or even both people involved will leave the organisation either while it is proceeding or soon after it is completed, sometimes with a lingering legal case against the organisation for failing to fulfill its duty of care or for other reasons. Even if they don't leave while it is proceeding it is very likely that at least one person involved will take time off due to stress.

This is understandable given the difficulty of being in the presence of someone about whom you have made a complaint or who has made a complaint about you alleging bullying. It is a consequence of the 'Prove it!' approach to such allegations. We can expect people to 'be professional', but they are also human beings and so their interactions will inevitably involve consideration of the ongoing investigation process rather than just the issues they are working on together.

This section is designed to help you support both people in finding a different way of responding and of understanding each other's perspective of their experiences. It is based on the practice of challenging, or exploring, the behaviour not the person, which is one of the underlying principles of mediation practice and is achieved through asking relevant questions to explore what happened and why it was difficult for the persons affected (both the person feeling bullied and the person accused) as well as to find out what would work better for them in the future.

The focus of the questions is entirely on providing an opportunity for those involved to create a better way forward in the future - they serve no other purpose.

It is important to recognise that in some situations the participants may be wary of engaging in such an exploration with someone who is also involved in investigation of the allegations. The person alleging bullying may feel it is trying to 'avoid tackling the bully' while the person accused of bullying may feel it is a 'sly attempt to prove I am the bully'. In such situations where the people involved feel wary or suspicious or unsafe it may be more appropriate to use a Mediator who is independent of the situation and who will maintain confidentiality regarding any discussions held with the people involved.

If only one participant wishes to engage with you in such an exploration, Conflict Coaching may be more appropriate to offer as a support for the other person.

But it may not always be necessary to draw upon outside help and so below I will describe what can be done without this.

Put simply the questions that can be asked are of the following type:

- What happened? (Shouting, swearing, ignoring, other...?)

- How did it affect you?

- What would you see as a different or better way of dealing with such situations in the future - by the other person, by yourself?

The point is to move away from the focus on 'proving /disproving bullying' and look at the detail of what actually happened that led to the difficulty or breakdown in the relationship. It may seem like this is already being done via the investigation route but the purpose is different here. No evidence or proof or opinion relating to what is said by those involved is needed. It is a process designed to help them think through what would improve the situation and to be able to express it and then consider how they can go about putting it in place

If this can be done with both people present that is preferable but if there are reasons why that's not possible, including any discomfort of your own at running such a meeting, it is fine to do the exploration with them separately. Whether together or separately the purpose is always to support them in thinking of other ways of doing things within their working relationship in the future that improve on how things were previously when the allegation of bullying and any other difficulties occurred.

On the next page is a 'question template' that can be used to help with appropriate questions or it could be used to create a form to give to both people and then the answers be passed between them if for any reason it is difficult for them to meet together. But this should not become the default option, it is always preferable if both people take responsibility for resolving the situation together and so ideally these exploratory questions can be used by a facilitator to support the person(s) involved in thinking through their answers in a meeting between them.

As you will see from the previous chapters, it is possible that those involved could have already asked themselves similar questions and even arranged to meet with each other to discuss their answers together. This option can be encouraged as much as possible if there are not other procedural reasons why it should not be so. However it should also only be done voluntarily so that it does not induce the 'hoop jumping' thinking that would undermine its effectiveness if people feel they have no choice about meeting with the other person and so just 'go through the motions'.

The Question template

Questions for the person alleging bullying:

Please think about the things that have happened/X has done which you say are bullying and then answer the following questions. (Answers can be written down or just kept 'in your head'.)

1. What has X done that is of concern to you? Please be more specific than saying 'bullying', describe what they have done, for example, shouted at you, swore at you, ignored you etc. If you feel they have been rude, for example, explain what they did that you felt was rude.

2. What would you like them to do instead? For example if they swear or shout when you make a mistake, or in a meeting with you, how would you prefer they do things? Please say more than 'Stop doing it!', please say what you would prefer them to do instead.

For example: 'When you shout/swear/bang the table in meetings I'd rather you said things more clearly because the shouting / swearing / table-banging doesn't help me to understand what it is you are saying and I worry that you are going to be aggressive or violent'

3. How can you communicate your ideas and requests to X if you haven't been able to so far? What would help you with doing that?

Questions for the person complained about:

Please think about the interactions you have had with Z and whether there are things you can see they may have considered to be bullying. You may not see it that way and the purpose of this questionnaire is not to prove either of you right or wrong, but to help you resolve things with them so it is a chance to look at how the situation can be improved.

Please consider your answers to the following questions. (Answers can be written down or just kept 'in your head'.)

1. What would you see as the difficult actions or behaviours that have happened in your working relationship with Z?

2. What actions or behaviours do you think Z may have interpreted as bullying? What was your intention in those situations? What, if anything, do you feel you could have done differently in those situations?

3. How can you communicate to Z these possible alternatives for your future working relationship if you haven't been able to so far? What would help you with doing that?

You will note that these questions are 'open' questions (starting with What, Why, Who, How, When, Where) through which you are supporting each person in creating their own answers to their situation rather than suggesting an answer, as would be the case if you said something like - 'Could you try....?' or 'Would it be a good idea to.....?' , 'Have you tried.....?' etc.

It is important that you stick to this approach of using open questions otherwise the risk is that those you are working with will be doing what you suggest as if it is a 'requirement', or because they believe they will gain favour in the investigative process. They may not feel able to turn down a suggestion from you and so they will then just be 'jumping through hoops' because they think that is what they have to do.

Using open questions ensures their answers are genuinely created by them and are not arising from your suggestion or attempts to 'fix it'. This means you are helping them to resolve the situation themselves. 'Fixing it' for them at this stage will prevent them seeing that it is possible to resolve their difficult situation themselves, which is ultimately what they will have to do in their future working relationship. If you try to fix it for them they are likely to repeatedly return to you in the future if there are other problems and may also expect you to 'police' their working relationship. It is therefore much more effective for all concerned if you stick with the use of open questions. (see more at http://www.communicationandconflict.com/questioning.html)

The participants may make requests of you when you ask the last question: 'What would help you with that?' with regard to how they could communicate their ideas for a better working relationship and it may be that you can provide a room for them to talk or sit with them while they talk, or help them in another way that they identify.

Chapter 6: Objections to this approach

One of the things I would like to emphasise about the approach suggested within this book is that is based on direct observation of the ways in which I have seen people resolve their difficulties over bullying and harassment within and beyond mediation and/or conflict coaching, although not exclusively via these processes. Sometimes people have simply decided for themselves to take a different approach than the 'Prove it!' approach of allegation followed by investigation.

So this isn't a psychological theory that I am setting against other theories. You will note there are no academic references quoted relating to 'models of behaviour', or 'conflict types', nor analytical questionnaires to be given to people prior to supporting them in order to 'diagnose' them. The Question template serves an entirely different purpose to that - it is designed to help those involved be reflective and creative in response to their difficulties, not to find something out about them or to analyse or investigate them.

Because it is not based on a theoretical model but on observation of 'what is' within resolved situations of workplace conflict the approach can be responded to by some as if it is a little naive and therefore subject to a range of objections. I will set out below some of the objections I have come across in order to give my best explanation of why I think the approach meets the challenges they present, again, based on where I have seen it happen.

Objection 1: Once the bullying investigation has started it's too late to use this approach

I would strongly disagree with this view as it can in fact be the time at which people are more likely to want an alternative approach. When they start to realise how stressful the investigative process is and they experience awkwardness at work because of the ongoing complaint, people can become much more open to the possibilities of an alternative approach. If they are finding that their view is not able to be proven and agreed with in the way they hoped - whether the person who feels bullied or the person accused, they may be more willing to consider an approach that enables the creation of a more positive future relationship instead of pursuing a dredging-up of the past, providing details and records and personal accounts of what happened for scrutiny and cross questioning.

Objection 2: What's the point? They won't be interested in improving things.

This obviously risks becoming a self-fulfilling prophecy and becomes a question of whom, if anyone, moves first. If both people assume the other will not be interested in pursuing an approach that is not looking to blame but to create a better way forward, then nothing can happen. But if just one person decides it is an alternative option worth pursuing then it starts a ball rolling that allows for exploration of other ways of responding that do not lead to the same difficulties that existed previously.

This is a process that can benefit enormously from just one of the people involved looking for alternative ways of working with the other person. A 'sub-objection' if that should occur could be, 'Why should I be the one doing the work?' and of course the answer is 'Well you don't have to be, but if you don't the other alternative is that which you have already experienced as stressful and frustrating, so ultimately the point is you are doing it because it benefits you and has potential side-benefits for the other person. But first and foremost it helps you!'

Objection 3: "This is ridiculous - they need to be punished for what they have done!"

If anyone feels strongly enough that this is true, possibly because there has been serious misconduct or physical assault in some form then of course they have a right to pursue that via an adversarial process that leads to punishment. But if that is not likely to be a guaranteed outcome and there are many counter-allegations against them that mean a clear outcome is unlikely then the objection risks being a block to creating a way forward that does not require punishment and which leads to a more positive working relationship in the future. The alternative is a working relationship which is extremely likely to end as a consequence of an investigative approach, whatever the findings of the investigation.

This is, in my experience, more likely to be an objection expressed by those who are supporting the person who feels bullied than the person themselves. It is an understandable view given that they have seen the impact of the situation on someone they care about or are supporting professionally, but if they are able to persuade the person not to try it, it can ultimately close the door on a more positive outcome than is likely via an approach seeking punishment. As has been mentioned previously it is not suggested the right to make a complaint is excluded when this approach is taken. Both can be progressed simultaneously if the individual and/or their organisation wish to do so.

Objection 4: "I've told them already, what's the point of saying it again, they already know?"

On the occasions when this objection has occurred and I have explored what the person feels they 'told' the other person (whether the person who feels bullied or the person alleged to be bullying) it has usually been an accusation or a denial ('Stop bullying me' - response: 'I'm not bullying you'). As described previously complaints and accusations usually involve the use of the label 'bully' or referral to the ambiguous concept of 'bullying' and so very little, if any, exploration of the actions and behaviours considered to be bullying occurs as the immediate response is simply denial. And so things remain stuck. The approach described in this book is not about 'telling' someone something, it is about discussing and exploring with a view at all times to at least acknowledge that someone has experienced an action or behaviour as difficult in some way and conversely to acknowledge that the person whose behaviour or act is being discussed may not have intended it that way.

'Telling' is one-way, it is not a discussion or a question or a request as described. A complaint or accusation immediately places the accuser in the role of victim. A descriptive and detailed account of the actions and behaviours and how they have been experienced by someone as unacceptable is an assertive communication that includes openness to hearing a different view and interpretation of those acts and behaviours. This is not communication by a victim, it is communication by someone who is able to assert their right to request consideration of something they are troubled by.

Correspondingly, a response to this communication that is also open to discussion and consideration of different interpretations of what has happened is not the communication of a 'bully', it is the communication of someone who is open to learning and change but also willing to clarify their intentions and where necessary assert that they were appropriate.

Chapter 7: Conclusion

We cannot solve our problems with the same thinking we used when we created them

I gave this quote, usually attributed to Albert Einstein, at the start of the book as it truly reflects the vicious circle that most approaches to bullying lead to. It is also fitting to use it in this conclusion as a reminder of the problems with the current prevailing response to bullying allegations. As long as bullying is responded to in a way that could just as easily be seen as bullying according to the many different definitions ascribed to the concept, there will not be a way out of that circle.

Some who presently work as advocates for those who feel bullied have themselves felt bullied in their workplace in the past and not found the punitive approach to have worked to their satisfaction. For many with this experience however their pursuit is one of greater determination to 'make it work' for those they work with who also feel bullied rather than consider whether the approach they pursued was ever an effective way of dealing with it in the first place.

Where this is so, it perpetuates the 'Find or become a bigger bully to bully the bully' thinking that has led to the dead ends that many bullying allegations arrive at. There is of course more that organisations and their leaders can do to improve the approaches taken to situations where bullying is alleged, but to devote more and more time and resources to an approach that is clearly not working for the majority of people who go through it is a direction that leads to the 'two steps forward three steps back' experience that is present in most situations where it is adopted.

A lot of energy is devoted to the predominantly adversarial and inherently hypocritical response to bullying that exists in many workplaces. When as much energy can be devoted to supporting the constructive engagement of those affected by the situation in communicating more openly and creating different, more effective and mutually acceptable responses to their difficulties then more working relationships will be maintained where they previously would have ended, less time, money and resources will be devoted to employment tribunals at which organisations are accused of failing to fulfill their duty of care, and the increasingly present phenomenon of 'bullying in the workplace' will finally start to subside.

Insanity: doing the same thing over and over again and expecting different results. **- also attributed to Albert Einstein.**

Or, you may prefer:

If you keep doing what you've always done you'll keep getting what you always got **- Anonymous.**

Thank you for reading this book.

If you enjoyed it and found it useful please leave a review at the retailer where you purchased it.

About the Author

Alan Sharland has been a mediator for 20 years and has worked in a range of mediation roles including the setting up and being Director of a community mediation service in West London, UK and now his own business CAOS Conflict Management. He has worked in various areas of dispute resolution including workplace disputes, neighbour disputes, community group difficulties, health service complaints, student complaints, special educational needs disputes and also group disputes in a variety of different contexts. He has written for mediate.com the world's largest mediation community website and written and provided webinars and podcasts for the Association for Talent Development (ATD) in relation to workplace engagement and effective responses to conflict.

While Director of Hillingdon Community Mediation, Alan and colleagues developed the UK's first publicly available Conflict Coaching service and he now continues to develop the model used to provide this through CAOS Conflict Management. He also helped Brunel University in West London to set up the first in-house Conflict Coaching service within a UK university.

Alan also provides training and webinars on effective communication and conflict resolution practice for organisations and individuals.

Other books by this author:

The Guide to the Principles of Effective Communication and Conflict Resolution - contact Alan for details - see next section.

The CAOS Conflict Management Conflict Coaching Clients Handbook - contact Alan for details.

Connect with Alan Sharland

Thank you for reading my book! Here are my social media contacts in case you would like to make contact:

CAOS Conflict Management on Facebook:

https://www.facebook.com/CAOS.Conflict.Management

Follow me on Twitter:

http://twitter.com/alan_sharland

Subscribe to my blog:

http://caotica.caos-conflict-management.co.uk

Connect on LinkedIn:

https://www.linkedin.com/pub/alan-sharland/14/84/a90

Visit my websites:

http://www.communicationandconflict.com

http://www.caos-conflict-management.co.uk

Please email me with any questions you have about this book or our work at CAOS Conflict Management:

alan@caos-conflict-management.co.uk